Born in Paris, CATHERINE ALLEGRE-PAPADACCI *teaches history and geography in a French school. Passionately interested in cross stitching, she has been embroidering for fifteen years during which time she began to create her own designs.*
She has a very personal and refined style. Her care for detail, her technical skill and wonderful sense of colour can be seen in the work she does for the finest magazines. In this, her first book, she shares with us her great passion for cross stitching.

CROSS STITCH

W O R K S T A T I O N

WORKSTATION *is a new concept comprising*
all the elements you need to commence
the art of Cross Stitching.

The first 48 pages of this book offer a full colour
introduction to cross stitching, and show you how to achieve
beautiful designs with easy to follow instructions.
At the back of the book are pages of templates, so you can
practise and carry out the projects illustrated in the book.

CATHERINE ALLEGRE-PAPADACCI

PRODUCED IN ASSOCIATION WITH

A DESIGN EYE BOOK

First published in the UK in 1995 by Design Eye Ltd.
The Corn Exchange, Market Square,
Bishops Stortford HERTS CM23 3XF

© 1994 Design Eye Holdings Ltd.

ISBN 1 872700 42 X

The Design Eye Team

Michael Tout
Lee Robinson
Aline Serra Littlejohn
Sally Symes
Joanne Coles

With thanks to Dorothea Hall
Photography by Richard Nourry and Jean-Paul Paireault,
pages 32 and 24 by Paul Forrester
Illustrations by Gerald Quinsat
Charts: DMC

Sampler on Page 4 from the 'Permin Collection',
linen cloth, 45 cm x 54 cm (20 in x 16 in), DMC archives.
Sampler on pages 36–37 30 gauge linen stitched over two fabric threads,
50 cm x 40 cm (20 in x 16 in)

Manufactured in China

CONTENTS

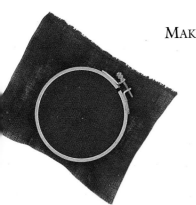

Sampler from the 'PERMIN collection', linen cloth 45 cm x 54 cm (18 in x 22 in).

INTRODUCTION

*C*ROSS STITCH IS ONE OF *the oldest forms of embroidery practised throughout the world. It is also the simplest and most common type of embroidery and, as its name implies, consists of two diagonal stitches placed one over the other so as to cross in the middle.*

Cross stitching, perhaps due to its simplicity, has remained popular for centuries, continuously enriching the heritage of ladies' 'fancy work' – as embroideries were called in Victorian and Edwardian times. For many years, its utilitarian and decorative functions were combined, mainly in beautifully designed names and monograms used to adorn the garments of a bride's trousseau, and so on.

Traditionally, little girls learned how to read, write and embroider all at the same time. These practice pieces, which came to be known as 'samplers', may have included a prayer, a proverb, an alphabet and numerals which, gradually, were embellished with innumerable small motifs and, possibly, a decorative border, along with the name and age of the young embroideress.

In Europe and North America, over the past fifteen years, there has been an astonishing growth of interest in cross stitch embroidery – one has only to look through women's magazines to see this. The types of projects that can be made are as equally varied and numerous as the occasions on which they can be given, and range from household furnishings to personalized gifts for family and friends (such as birthdays and weddings), through holiday events (including Christmas and Eastertime), to very special occasions like Mother's Day and Father's Day.

With a little patience and a needle and thread, stitch by stitch you will soon learn how to cross stitch pumpkins and rabbits, for example, on to some wonderful projects. You will find that, amid the noise and bustle of the day, it is quite calming and therapeutic to allow yourself a few moments with your embroidery. So, whether you are aged seven or 77, and whether you have one or more hours to spare: go ahead and cross stitch!

EQUIPMENT

BEFORE YOU BEGIN TO EMBROIDER, make sure you have all the
necessary equipment to hand. When you are not working on your
embroidery, keep it covered, or in a workbag, to protect it from dust.

THREADS

There are several types of thread available for cross stitch embroidery.
Essentially, the thickness of the embroidery thread is determined by
the weight of the embroidery fabric and the openness of the weave.
Six-stranded embroidery cottons are popular; they can easily be
separated and used singly or in different multiples as required.

Evenweave fabrics
Reading from right to left: large open checked Hardanger
fabric; guest towel with an integrated band of evenweave
fabric; honeycomb hand towel with combined Aida band;
pink and green 'gingham check' evenweave tea towels;
16 and 18 gauge Aida fabric—also available in
several other gauges and colours; natural
(unbleached) and pewter coloured linens.

Braids
Evenweave braids in
various colours and
widths ranging from
2.5 cm (1 in) to
13 cm (5 in).

There are over 400 different colours of embroidery
threads available for cross stitching including
six-stranded cotton, coton à broder,
pearl and metal threads.

THE FABRICS

Choosing a fabric

Your choice of fabric should depend largely on the intended purpose of the project and the amount of time you will have to work it. If you have only a short time, then perhaps your choice should be Aida fabric since this is woven in blocks of threads, which are quicker to work than single threads of linen or cotton, for example. On the other hand, if you are planning to make a special present, where time is not important, then perhaps a traditional linen should be your choice.

Types of evenweave fabrics

Cross stitch embroidery is usually worked on an evenweave fabric: that is any fabric with the same number of threads counted in both directions, usually over 2.5 cm (1 in). These fabrics are known by their count or gauge: the higher the number, the finer the fabric and thread, and the smaller the stitch will be. Of course, on finer fabrics, stitches may be worked over 2, 3 or more threads.

Linens are traditionally used for cross stitch embroidery, and are available in a range of gauges and colours: natural and antique finishes being most popular and traditional. Most linens are woven with a single weave except for Hardanger, which has a double weave, and huckaback, which is woven in groups of threads and forms a checked effect similar to that of Aida fabrics.

Evenweave fabrics are also made from cotton and cotton/linen mixes, such as Zweigart's Linda, Lugana, Davosa and Quaker cloth respectively. These names denote the particular gauge, and all varieties are made in a range of colours. Cotton Aida fabric is also produced in a wide range of colours and gauges.

Household Linens
Household linens made especially for cross stitching include cotton hand towels which have a border of Aida fabric, linen or linen mixed tea towels, pot holders and table napkins.

ACCESSORIES

The following examples are just a selection of the many ways in which cross stitch can be used to decorate accessories for the whole family: Christmas stockings, jampot covers, paperweights, spectacle cases and cushions.

Hoops

An embroidery hoop is a useful accessory. It stretches the ground fabric evenly which helps you to make regular stitches with an even tension. Hoops (and frames) with or without table clamps are available in sizes ranging from 10 cm (4 in) to 60 cm (24 in) across. A 15 cm (6 in) hoop is a popular size.

Scissors

You will need a pair of small, sharp-pointed embroidery scissors for neatening threads. To prevent spoiling the blades, keep them solely for this purpose. So that they are handy, some people thread them onto a ribbon and hang them around the neck.

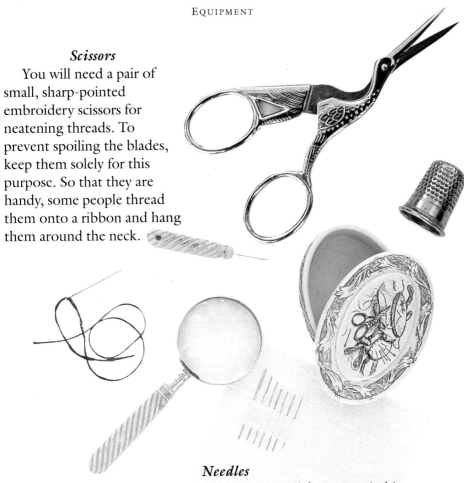

Needles

Round-ended tapestry needles should be used for cross stitching on evenweave fabrics, where they will move easily through the fabric mesh without piercing it. They are available in sizes 18-25: choose the size according to the fabric weight—the finer it is, the smaller the eye should be. To cross stitch by the 'waste fabric' method you may need to use a crewel needle and thimble, depending on the fineness of the ground fabric.

General accessories

In addition to the items mentioned above, you may need a small box for storing the threads, a needle-threader, a magnetic needle box, a support for holding the chart, a magnetic board, a pencil and ruler with a magnifying glass, and graph paper.

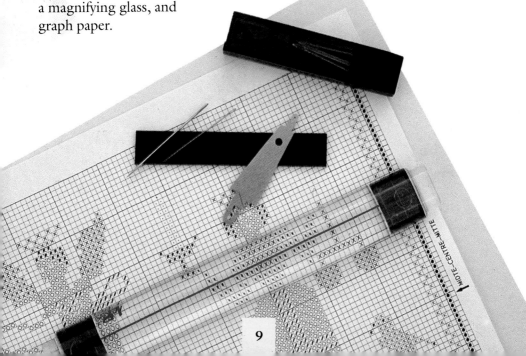

SOURCES OF INSPIRATION

The sources of inspiration for cross stitch embroidery are numerous, and can be most unexpected. As almost any design that is charted on a grid can be adapted for cross stitching, we may, for example, be inspired by a tile design, a knitted motif, or a geometric carpet pattern; illustrations in newspapers and magazines, and the many embroidery books that are currently produced, as well as those which are now out of print but can be seen in libraries, and so on.

Books on historical textiles, and ethnic embroideries in particular, are excellent sources of inspiration for cross stitch. We may be attracted to a certain border design, alphabet, or floral motif, for example, all of which may be combined into a design, such as the garden sampler on pages 36–38, or motifs can be used singly on projects of your own choice—the permutations are endless!

In addition to the abundant literature on embroidery and textiles now available in bookshops and craft suppliers, books on other specific subjects such as calligraphy, mosaics, wild and cultivated flowers; making gifts for Christmas or for children (where cross stitch projects are included) may all be inspirational.

There are a number of weekly and monthly magazines available which deal partly or entirely with cross stitching—and may also be valuable sources of inspiration. Many of these magazines promote contemporary designers whose names the reader will eventually recognize since they employ the current practice of signing their published creations!

It is also a good idea to look at other craft techniques which use designs charted on graph paper, such as lacemaking and crochet. You will see just how simple it would be to cross stitch a blouse to match the motif on a cardigan, for instance. Many needlepoint designs can also be adapted to cross stitch, especially where they are worked in petit point or other similar small stitches. Here, the needlepoint backgrounds would be left unworked, allowing the evenweave fabric to show.

Experiment with these suggestions and enjoy your own quest for new sources of inspiration.

Creazione Anna Ricotti dalla
serie le "filastrocche di Marianna"

11

STITCH DIAGRAMS

S IMPLE CROSS STITCH consists of two diagonal stitches placed one over the other, which cross in the middle. Make sure that each stitch and successive rows cross in the same direction throughout the embroidery.

How to work cross stitch

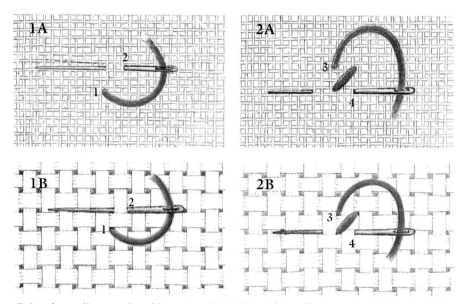

Bring the needle out at 1 and insert it at 2.   *Bring the needle out at 3 and insert it at 4.*

Working horizontal rows in two stages

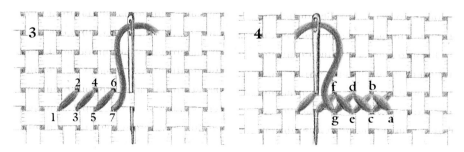

Stitch diagonally starting from the bottom left (1) towards the upper right corner (2), and repeat following the numerical order.

At the end of the row, bring the needle out at the bottom right corner (a), and insert it at the top left (b). Repeat following in alphabetical order.

Working single stitches in rows across

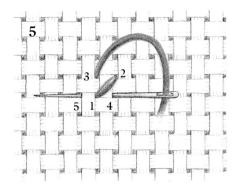

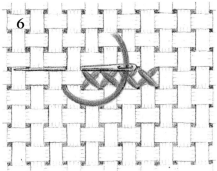

Bring the needle out at 1, insert it at 2, bring out at 3, and re-insert at 4. Begin new stitch at 5.

Continue along the row working from right to left, completing each stitch before proceeding to the next one.

Working single stitches in vertical rows

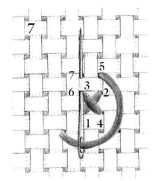

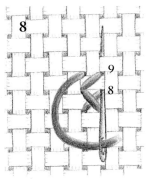

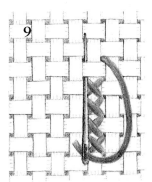

Work the first cross stitch following the number sequence. Bring the needle out at 5, insert at 6 and bring out again at 7.

Re-insert the needle at 8 and bring out at 9.

Continue along the row working bottom to top, completing each stitch before proceeding to the next one.

Working vertical rows in two stages

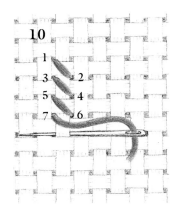

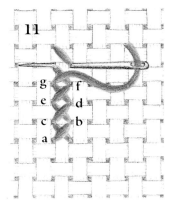

Work diagonal stitches starting from top left corner (1), towards bottom right corner (2), following numerical order.

At the end of the row, bring the needle out at the bottom left corner (a) insert at top right (b). Complete the row following alphabetical order.

Working diagonally upwards

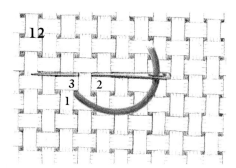

Bring the needle out at 1, insert it at 2 and bring it out at 3.

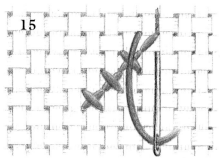

Insert the needle at 4 and bring it out at 5.

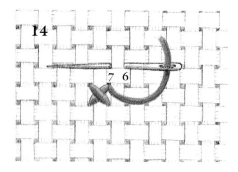

Insert the needle at 6 and bring it out at 7.

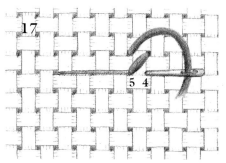

Continue working diagonally upwards to end of row, completing each stitch as you go.

Working diagonally downwards

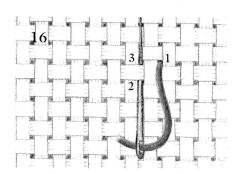

Bring the needle out at 1, insert it at 2 and bring it out at 3.

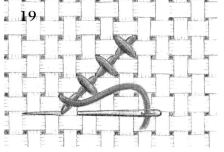

Insert the needle at 4 and bring it out at 5.

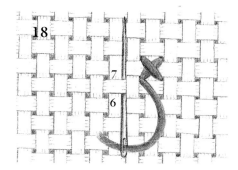

Insert the needle at 6 and bring it out at 7.

Continue working diagonally downwards completing each stitch as you go.

Backstitch

Backstitch is often used in cross stitch embroidery to emphasize certain parts of a design, in continuous straight or diagonal lines.

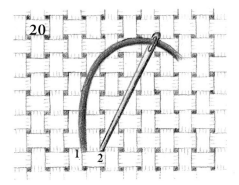

Bring the needle out at 1 and insert it to the right at 2.

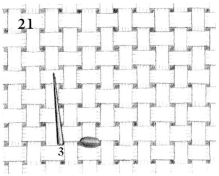

Bring the needle out at 3; the stitch on the back is therefore twice as long as the first stitch (1 to 2).

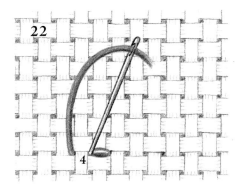

Reinsert the needle at 4, which is the starting point, 1.

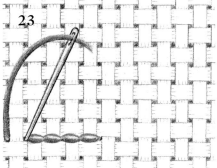

Continue in the same way, following the weave of the fabric and your particular chart.

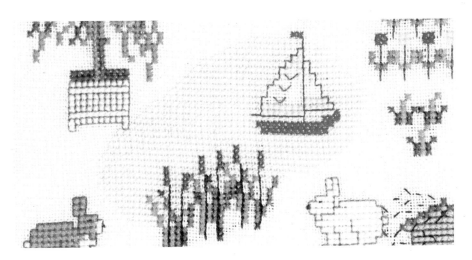

Half cross stitch is a simple diagonal stitch used mainly in needlepoint. In cross stitch embroidery it can be used to give the transparent effect of sky or water for example; in this garden, the pond is embroidered with half cross stitch.

CHARTS

HOW TO READ A CHART

Designs for cross stitch embroidery are drawn on graph paper, mostly in
black and white, and using symbols to represent the colours. Each
square on the chart represents one cross stitch worked over one or more
fabric intersections (as instructed with each project), and each symbol

represents a colour. In
order to centre your
design accurately on the
fabric, work outwards
from the middle. Before
stitching, mark the centre
of your chart by
following the centre

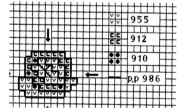

arrows, as shown on the
charts opposite, and then
count the number of
squares and the
corresponding number of
fabric threads.

  For this reason, cross
stitch embroidery is often
called 'counted' cross
stitch.

  Sometimes there are
straight lines on diagrams
which either outline the
motifs or are
superimposed on them.
These lines are usually
backstitched, in a

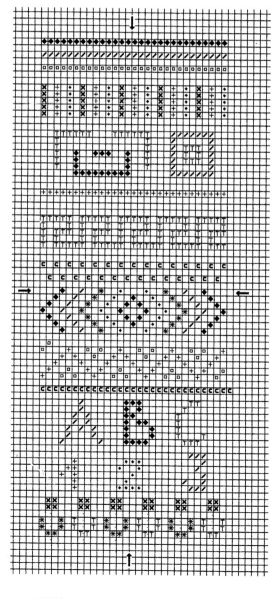

contrasting colour to the design and with fewer threads than the cross stitch (one thread instead of two for instance).

Embroidery thread organizer

On larger pieces of embroidery that involve many different colours, it is useful to make a card on which you can fix each thread opposite its symbol. You can find ready-made cards of this sort in haberdashery stores, otherwise a small piece of cardboard with holes in it will do the job. Remember also to write down the number of each colour in case you have to buy some more! The first reading of the chart should be to decipher the colour symbols, and then to mark the centre of it.

In order to fit larger designs on the page, the charts may have to be reduced in scale. In which case, it is helpful to photocopy them, enlarging them to scale so that the symbols can be seen more easily.

You can also use the colour photograph of the embroidery to check the details, especially backstitching, which may not show up easily on the black and white chart.

FIRST STEPS

HOW TO BEGIN A PROJECT

If you wish to work a project where the specific fabric gauge is not given, first select your cross stitch design, already charted on graph paper, and then choose the appropriate fabric. Your choice will depend on the purpose of the project, the suitability of the design, and your personal taste.

Remember that evenweave fabrics have a certain number of threads per centimetre (inch)—the gauge— and that one square on the chart represents one cross stitch.

Before cutting out your fabric, calculate how big the finished motif will be by counting the squares on the chart, (see the pumpkin opposite, for example) and then counting the equivalent number of threads on your fabric: in the case of Aida fabric, count the intersecting blocks.

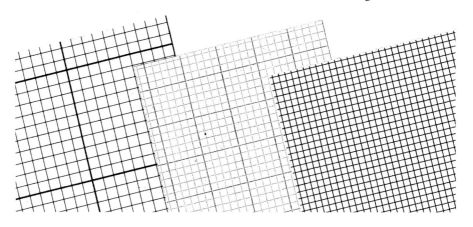

Above: different types of graph paper.

Below: examples of cross stitch embroidery on different kinds of fabric.

 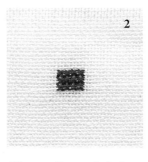 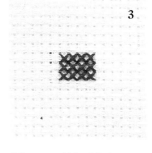

30 gauge linen, stitched over one fabric thread.

30 gauge linen, stitched over two fabric threads.

11 gauge Aida fabric, stitched over each block.

The finished size of the pumpkin motif will be:

- On the linen, stitched over a single thread:
  22 : 30 = 2 cm (¾ in) wide
  18 : 30 = 1.5 cm (⁹⁄₁₆ in) high
- On the linen, stitched over two fabric threads:
  22 : 30 = 4 cm (1⁹⁄₁₆ in) wide
  18 : 30 = 3 cm (1¹³⁄₁₆ in) high
- On the Aida fabric stitched over one block:
  22 : 11 = 5 cm (2 in) wide
  18 : 11 = 4 cm (1⅝ in) high

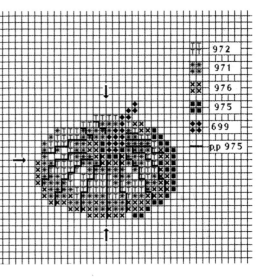

The big pumpkin: 22 squares wide, 18 squares high.

Once you have calculated these measurements accurately, add a further 5cm (2in) all round for stretching it in a hoop (frame). Cut out the fabric to size, carefully cutting along the threads to give a straight edge.

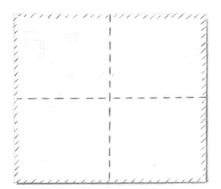

Preparing the fabric

Before you begin to embroider, steam-press the fabric under a cloth to remove any creases. Then, overcast the edges to prevent them from fraying. Using contrasting tacking cotton, mark the centre of your fabric both vertically and horizontally with lines of tacking stitches. Once the embroidery is completed, remove these tacked lines.

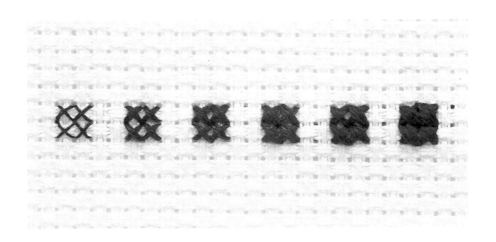

Organize the necessary embroidery threads (see page 17). Mark the middle of the chart with pencil if necessary. Choose the appropriate number of threads suitable for your chosen fabric. Work a few test stitches first, remembering that the stitches should be clearly visible but cover the ground fabric well. (The example above shows four stitches worked with 1, 2, 3, 4, 5 and 6 threads. 2 or 3 are recommended.)

Using a hoop

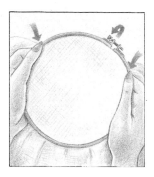 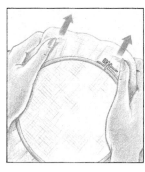 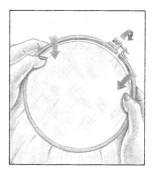

Place the area of fabric to be embroidered on the inner ring and press the outer ring over it with the tension screw released.

Stretch the fabric outwards, and make sure the fabric grain stays straight: tighten the tension screw.

To remove the finished embroidery, loosen the screw and push the inner ring downwards.

Handling the threads

It is important to handle the threads with care to prevent them losing their sheen. An average workable length is between 40cm (16in) and 50cm (20in): longer lengths will twist and knot in use. If you haven't made a thread organizer, see page 17, keep the labels with the number of the colours in case you need to buy more.

Separating six-stranded embroidery thread: cut off a workable length and remove the number of threads you require by pulling out one thread at a time.

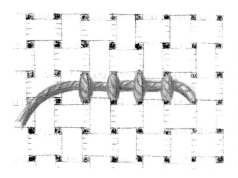

In cross stitch embroidery, do not make knots when beginning or fastening off a thread, as they would appear in relief on the right side when the work is pressed. Begin the first stitch from the wrong side leaving 2.5cm (1in) of thread hanging from the back and make the first stitches over it, thus holding it in place.

An alternative technique involves using several strands: cut off 90 cm (35 in) to 102 cm (40 in) of thread, fold it in half and thread the two ends through the needle—producing a loop at the other end.

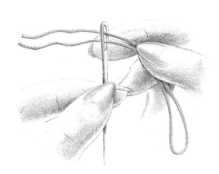

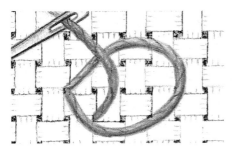

Work half a cross stitch and pull the needle through the loop at the back of the work. You can then continue with the embroidery without leaving loose threads.

This technique is useful for working very small areas of embroidery. In this case, adjust the length of thread in the needle: for example, 10 stitches would require 5cm (2in) of thread only. To finish, weave the thread under 5 or 6 stitches at the back. Cut off leaving just 6mm (¼ in) protruding.

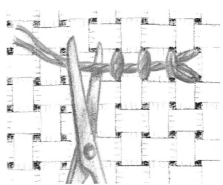

General advice
Cross stitch embroidery is usually done by starting in the middle of the fabric and working outwards. On fine openweave fabrics, it is important not to strand the embroidery threads across the back of the work, as they will show on the right side. When stitches of the same colour are far away from each other, it is better to fasten them off and start again. Otherwise, weave the thread under a few stitches on the back of the embroidery, which should be as neat as the front.

For best results, it is important to take time in preparing your embroidery, checking and, if necessary, cross-checking that you have counted the squares correctly, that you have the correct fabric and thickness of thread, for example. This may prevent costly mistakes. Where there are full instructions given with a project, read them very carefully before starting.

Your first embroidery
This is designed as a small sampler and involves a series of exercises suitable for beginners to cross stitch. Using the materials supplied, complete the embroidery and mount it as a picture or use it as a bookmark.

Starting at the top left, use two strands of thread for the cross stitching and one for the tulip stems.

These pretty household linens, with their simple cross stitch designs, are both easy and quick to work.

'Cuisine' tea towel

The design is worked on a band of evenweave fabric in a single colour.

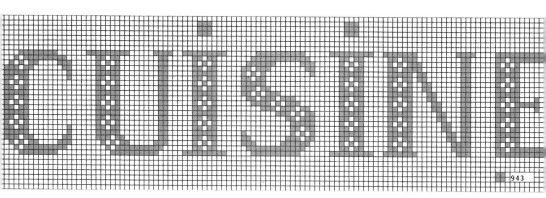

The embroidery
Mark the centre of the chart both ways and corresponding lines on the Aida band. Tack a line across to position the bottom of the letters, and cross stitch using three strands of thread. Press on the wrong side.

Materials
- *1 green tea towel with band of Aida fabric*
- *3 skeins of DMC stranded embroidery cotton 943*

'Leeks and pumpkins' tea towel

Leek and pumpkin motifs cross stitched in naturalistic colours are repeated across the tea towel on a band of Aida fabric. An alternative design of leeks and lettuce is shown below.

Materials
- 1 yellow tea towel
- DMC stranded embroidery cotton, 1 skein of each colour:

Pumpkin
- green 699
- pale orange 972
- orange 971
- brown orange 976
- brown 975
- outlining 975

Leek
- off-white
- lime green 472
- pale green 3347
- green 3346
- dark green 3345
- outline: very dark green 895
- stalk and root outline: ochre 729

See charts on page XII

The embroidery

Mark the centre of each chart both ways, see page XII, and corresponding lines on the Aida band. Tack a line across to position the bottom of the vegetables. Using three strands and, starting 9 blocks in from the left, work a leek, and 18 blocks away, work a pumpkin. Repeat across the band. If needed, adjust the spaces to fit your tea towel. Outline the motifs using two strands. Press on the wrong side.

'Leeks and Lettuce' tea towel

Materials
- 1 blue tea towel with band of Aida fabric
- DMC stranded embroidery cotton. 1 skein of each colour:

Lettuce
- pale green 955
- bright green 912
- green 910
- outlines: very dark green 986

Leeks
(see previous tea towel)

The embroidery

Mark the fabric and charts as for the previous tea towel. At each side of the vertical centre and 20 blocks away, embroider a leek. Count 12 blocks between the leaves and work a second leek. Count another 12 blocks and work a lettuce, using the same number of strands as before. Press on the wrong side.

Seed sachets

Repeating the same vegetable motifs as before, make these three delightful seed sachets from a natural linen braid decoratively edged with dark green, see Equipment on pages 6–7. Keep your seeds safe by tying the tops of the sachets with matching green ribbon.

Making the sachets

Materials
For one bag:
- 50 cm (20 in) of 24 gauge natural linen braid, 13 cm (5 in) wide with green edging
- 30 cm (12 in) green ribbon, 6 mm (¼ in) wide
- DMC stranded embroidery cotton, 1 skein of each colour:

Leek
- off-white
- lime green 472
- pale green 3347
- green 3346
- dark green 3345

Pumpkin
- green 699
- pale orange 972
- orange 971
- outlining brown 975

Radish
- red 326
- bright green 906
- dark green 904

Work the lettering centrally on the braid, placing its top edge 10 cm (4 in) in from the short side. Work each stitch over two fabric threads using two strands in the needle. Fold the braid in half and then embroider your chosen vegetable in the centre. Outline with one strand. Hem both short sides and press. Re-fold and stitch the two sides together. Fill and secure the top with ribbon.

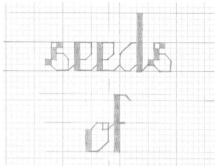

Tablemats

For eating alfresco, make these four colourful tablemats to complement your garden table. The designs use all four vegetable motifs, and concludes the first series of cross stitch exercises.

Materials

For one tablemat:
- *43 cm x 33 cm (17 in x 13 in) of 30 gauge white linen, plus seam allowances*
- *DMC stranded embroidery cotton, 1 skein of each colour:*

Pumpkin, Leek and Radish, *see the seed sachets, opposite*

Lettuce
- *pale green 993*
- *green 992*
- *dark green 991*
- *outline: very dark green 500*

Making the tablemats

Cut out the tablemat along the straight threads of the fabric. Following the chart, where each square represents one stitch worked over two fabric threads and using two strands, work the motifs as shown, placing them 5 cm (2 in) inside the top corners of the tablemat. Use one strand for outlining. Hem the edges, see pages 42–43, and press on the wrong side. Complete the remaining tablemats.

ENLARGING
OR REDUCING

"**O**NCE UPON A TIME, there were three bears. The first one was big, the second one was medium-sized, the third one was small..." A motif can be made bigger or smaller quite simply by stitching in finer or heavier gauge fabric. The following three 'bear' projects will show you how.

'Baby bear' cardigan

In order to use a cross stitch motif on a non-evenweave fabric, such as the baby's cardigan, a technique called the 'waste method' is used, whereby the motif is transferred to the garment by stitching through evenweave fabric, which is first secured to the garment, and then pulling away the threads.

First tack the evenweave fabric firmly to the garment. Stretch both fabrics in a hoop and, following the chart, stitch through both layers, but do not pull the stitching too tight. For this, you will probably need a crewel needle. Complete the embroidery and then gently pull each thread away, using tweezers, if necessary.

The embroidery

Tack the evenweave fabric in position. Mark corresponding centre lines on the chart and fabric and, using one strand throughout, cross stitch over each fabric thread. Remove the threads and press.

Materials
- *1 flannel cardigan*
- *10 cm (4 in) square of 20 gauge linen*
- *DMC stranded embroidery cotton, 1 skein of each colour (see the opposite page)*

'Mummy bear' brooch

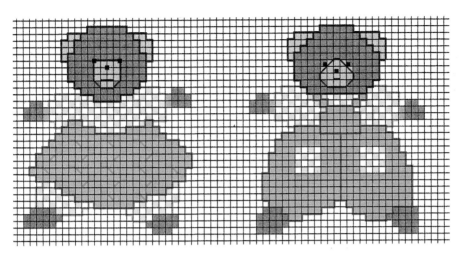

Materials

- 1 special brooch for embroidery 5 cm (2 in) across
- 10 cm (4 in) of 26 gauge white linen
- DMC stranded embroidery cotton, 1 skein of each colour:
- light brown 437
- brown 435
- outline: dark brown 433
- yellow 744
- blue 809
- outline: 783
- orange 742
- black 310
- outline: dark blue 798

The embroidery

Embroider the bear motif centrally on the fabric, working each stitch over one fabric thread, with one strand in the needle. Press. Assemble the brooch following the maker's instructions.

'Baby bear' bib

The embroidery

Mark corresponding centre lines both ways on the chart and the Aida band. Following the chart, and using two strands of thread, work a boy and girl bear 5 blocks away from the centre. Outline with one strand. Press on the wrong side.

Materials

- 1 bib with Aida border
- DMC stranded embroidery cotton, 1 skein of each colour: see 'Mummy bear' brooch and add green 913 for the stalk of the orange flowers

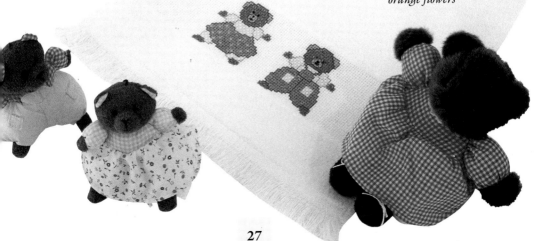

In the previous examples, the bear motifs were made bigger and smaller by stitching them on fabrics of different gauges, but designs can also be made bigger by increasing the number of threads the stitch is worked over. The initial below is worked over two threads, see page IX for the remaining alphabet.

'C' pendant

The embroidery

Work the initial using two strands. Press and mount it in the pendant.

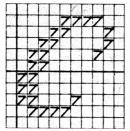

Materials
- *1 oval pendant*
- *a small piece of 30 gauge linen cloth, 20 threads per inch*
- *an oddment of coloured thread, DMC stranded embroidery cotton: 826 used here*

Hand towel

Materials
- *hand towel with Aida border*
- *DMC stranded embroidery cotton, 1 skein of each colour:*
- *pale pink 353*
- *pink 352*
- *blue-green 993*
- *dark blue-green 991*

The embroidery

Chart your initials, see page IX, leaving four threads between. Using three strands in the needle and placing them centrally on the Aida band, for each square, work two stitches over two threads. Work the borders at each side, 8 threads away, working over a single thread, using two strands. Press.

When a chart is enlarged, as in the last project, the outline may be too steeply stepped for a naturalistic subject, for example. In this case, the corners may need smoothing by adding or taking away squares. You will see by the rabbit motifs below what changes can be made.

'Rabbit and Lettuce' box

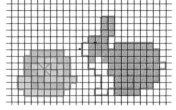

Materials
- 1 white porcelain box
- 1 small piece of white 30 gauge linen
- DMC stranded embroidery cotton, 1 skein of each colour:

Rabbit
- brown 3064
- white
- outline dark brown 632

Lettuce
- blue-green 993
- green 992
- dark green 991
- outline: very dark green 500

The embroidery
Using two strands, stitch over two threads and outline with one. Press and mount the embroidery in the lid, following the manufacturer's instructions.

'Big rabbit' cushion

Materials
- 28 cm x 20 cm (11 in x 8 in) of ecru Lugana
- 60 cm x 30 cm (24 in x 12 in) of checked cotton fabric
- 30 cm (12 in) square cushion pad
- DMC stranded embroidery cotton, 2 skeins of each colour:

- brown 3064
- dark brown 632
- white
- DMC stranded embroidery cotton, 1 skein of each colour:
- pink beige 950
- pink 353
- dark grey 3799

Making the cushion
Work the rabbit in the centre of the fabric. Using two strands, stitch over two threads, and outline with one. Press. Make a narrow turning on all sides, and stitch it to the cover.

See the chart on page XII.

BORDERS

Borders can be seen in many types of cross stitch designs:
traditional sampler, for example, are usually surrounded with a
border, which serves to emphasize the central subject. A border can also
be worked on evenweave braid, see pages 31–32.

A border design consists of smaller design units repeated in sequence,
which creates its own movement or geometrical rhythm.

Just about any subject is possible, as long as the design repeats in
shape and colour.

For instance, take the terracotta pots: there are six of them, divided
into two groups: round and straight. The simplest arrangement shown
below is of alternating straight and round pots, spaced equally apart.
They could also have been arranged in alternating pairs or, the same pot
repeated in a series of different colours. The unity here, however, is in
the use of the same colour. Braids are best for this type of border.

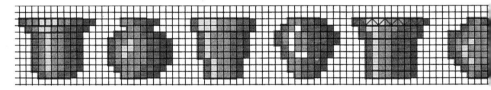

The rhythmic movement of a design can be changed by altering the
colour emphasis. In the examples shown below, you can see how the
flowing effect is made by the darker colour.

On the other hand,
if the vertical lines
are emphasized, the
movement becomes
more erratic.

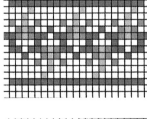
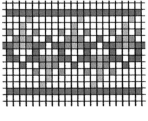

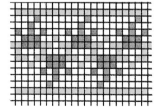
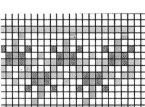
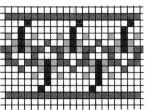

You can also experiment with the colour tones (warm or cold), their intensity (light or dark), and their relation to each other (primary, secondary or complementary), according to the desired effect.

The simplest way to stitch a border

Use the technique whereby each stitch is completed before moving on to the next and, if preferred, use more than one needle, so that all the colours are completed as you work along the border.

'Terracotta braid pots'

The embroidery

Using two strands in the needle, begin 10cm (4in) in at the left, and 9 blocks in from the bottom edge. Following the chart, repeat the series of six pots, according to the size of your braid, spacing them 19 blocks apart (counting from the bottom). Work each stitch over one block. Outline. Press.

Materials
- *15 gauge white Aida braid, 5 cm (2 in) wide, to size*
- *1 basket*
- *DMC stranded embroidery cotton, 1 skein of each colour:*
- *off-white*
- *pale orange 402*
- *burnt orange 921*
- *brown 918*
- *outlines: brown 918*

'Pots of plants' shelf edging

Materials
- *30 gauge white linen braid, blue edged, 8 cm (3 in) wide*
- *DMC stranded embroidery cotton, 1 skein of each colour:*

Pots
- *pale blue 827*
- *blue 826*
- *dark blue 824*
- *green for decoration 1 thread 943*
- *outline: 824*

Plants 1
- *greens 907, 906, 904*

Plants 2
- *greens 955, 911, 909*
- *orange 741*

Plants 3
- *branches 704, 702, 700*

Plants 4
- *472, 470, 937*
- *outline: 1 thread 937*

Plants 5
- *greens 704, 702, 700*
- *trunk 780*
- *outline: 1 thread 986*

Plants 6
- *greens 471, 937, 1 thread*

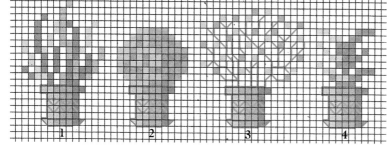

Plants 7
- *greens 955, 911, 909*
- *outline 909*

Plants 8
- *greens 907, 906, 904 for the stalks*
- *orange yellow 741, 743 for the flowers*

Making the shelf edging

Calculate how much braid you will need by measuring the shelf and allowing for a hem at each side. With two strands in the needle, and stitching over two threads, work the plant pots placing them 8 threads up from the bottom edge and 20 threads apart (between the saucers). Outline with one thread. Press and attach to your shelf with self-adhesive pads.

32

'Little boats' beaker

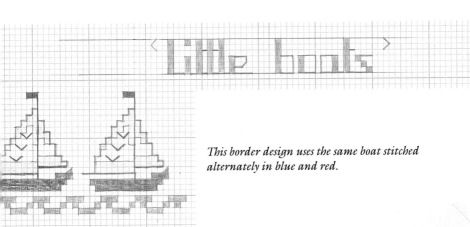

This border design uses the same boat stitched alternately in blue and red.

Materials
- 1 child's beaker
- 14 gauge white Aida Plus to fit around beaker
- DMC stranded embroidery cotton, 1 skein of each colour:
- red 321
- pale blue 747
- grey blue 334
- bright blue 797

Making the border design
Begin stitching the sea 2 blocks from the left side and 3 blocks from the bottom. Following the chart, complete the border using two threads. Outline with one thread.

CHARTING YOUR OWN MOTIF

1) Draw the subject without thinking of its application. Paint it.

2) Using tracing-paper, transfer the drawing onto the appropriate graph paper. When choosing graph paper remember that the finer the grid, the more shades and tones there will be and the bigger the grid, the simpler and more stylized the drawing will become. Make several tests if needed. Here the graph paper has 12 squares per 2.5cm (1in).

3) Using a pencil, follow the outline of the drawing, adapting it to the grid. At the same time, outline the different colours.

4) Transfer this rough sketch onto another gird, using a finer pencil (2H), to get a cleaner drawing. Here the drawing has been outlined with Indian ink to obtain greater legibility (drawing A).

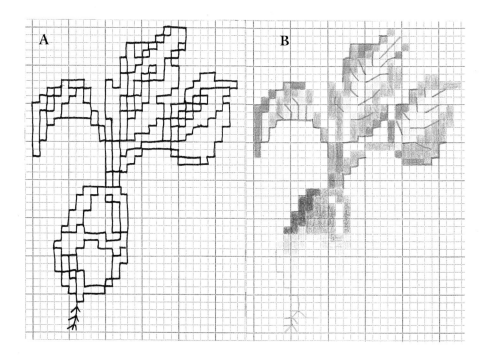

5) Colour the drawing. Coloured pencil crayons are particularly easy to use. They allow for different depths of colour, and can be erased in case of error. Certain brands are available in very wide ranges of colour. Remember to leave a few spots of white (stitched or not) to highlight the drawing (coloured drawing B).

6) If you wish, you can transcribe the finished chart into black and white (in which case you can also make photocopies, for instance), using a different symbol for each colour (black and white drawing C).

7) All you have to do now is to choose your thread colours from the DMC range and embroider your design.

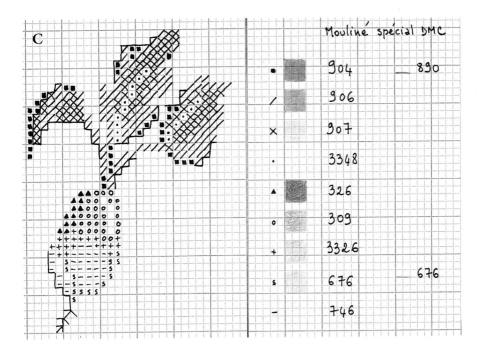

		Mouliné spécial DMC	
■		904	___ 890
/		906	
×		907	
•		3348	
▲		326	
o		309	
+		3326	
s		676	___ 676
–		746	

'Radish' potholder

Materials
- 1 potholder ready to embroider
- DMC stranded embroidery cotton, 1 skein of each colour:
- light pink 3326
- pink 309
- dark pink 326
- cream 746
- beige (roots and outline) 676
- lime green 3348
- bright green 907
- green 906
- dark green 904
- veins and outlines 890

The embroidery

Mark the centre of the potholder and the chart, see page 16. Using two strands, complete the embroidery. Press on the wrong side.

COMPOSITION

The definition of 'composition' is 'making a satisfactory product out of different elements'. The word 'satisfactory' immediately shows how subjective and personal any composition may be. Nevertheless, there are certain elementary rules to be followed concerning the balance and colour of the objects, as we will see in the following themes taken from the garden.

STARTING WITH SHAPES

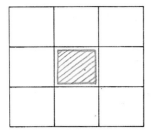 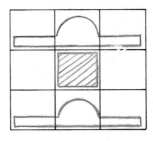 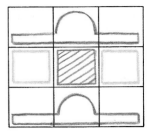

In this drawing, the alphabet is the principal theme, so it has been placed in the centre. To set it off, it has been framed at the top and bottom by two identical geometrical shapes, and also at the left and right.

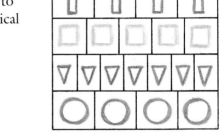

Once the area has been divided this way, the same idea of balance is used to fill the divisions with simple geometrical shapes, as shown in the diagram opposite.

a circle ○ for a pumpkin
a triangle ▽ for a radish
a square □ for a lettuce
and a rectangle with a star on top ▯ for a leek

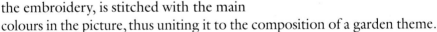

When the composition is pleasingly filled and well balanced, you can then choose the colours. Remember that colours can be warm or cold, light or dark or complementary. Use these different elements as a means of expressing your chosen theme.

In this example, the colours selected are light and bright to suggest a fresh atmosphere. The alphabet, which is the central part of the embroidery, is stitched with the main colours in the picture, thus uniting it to the composition of a garden theme.

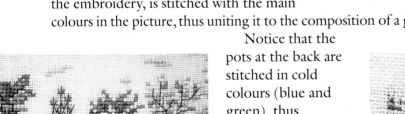

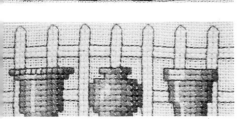

Notice that the pots at the back are stitched in cold colours (blue and green), thus emphasizing the distant effect, whereas the terracotta pots in warm colours emphasize closeness. See how the orange spots on the mother bear's dress sparkle, due to the complementary blue—without it, they may have gone unnoticed (see page 27).

38

Here are other examples of square compositions on checked cloth. The checks themselves give possible lines of composition. You can decide to put the motifs inside the squares or on the intersections and then choose the colours (light, medium or dark), according to your choice. Here the bee-hive has been placed so as to fill the darkest check, which is justified as the motif covers practically the whole square. On the other hand, the bees are stitched on white squares so that those parts of the wings that are not stitched appear to be transparent.

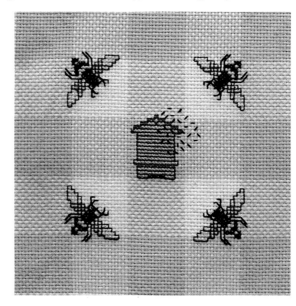

To break the rigidity of the woven checks, notice how the wings and legs of the bees run into the next squares, as does the roof of the beehive.

Lastly, to avoid the design being too symmetrical, a swarm of bees has been stitched to one side of the bee-hive.

The next two designs show other examples of classical composition, this time in a circle with a central design as the main element.

The first one uses a simple line in complementary colours (blue and orange) to surround a potted plant.

The second one uses tulips placed at angles, which gives the idea of a circle.

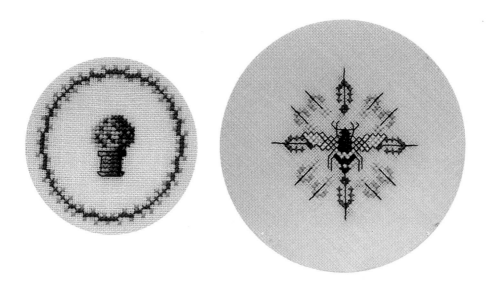

These are a few examples of how everyday things in your environment may be used to help you create your own designs.

Honey pot cover

Materials

- *15 cm (6 in) square of 16–18 gauge checked evenweave fabric*
- *60 cm (24 in) narrow deep yellow ribbon*
- *DMC stranded embroidery cotton, 1 skein of each colour:*

Beehive
- *beige 437*
- *brown 433*
- *outline: brown 433*
- *dark grey 3799 (2 lines)*

Bees
- *yellow 725*
- *black 310*
- *dark brown 938*
- *beige 677*
- *outline: brown 433*

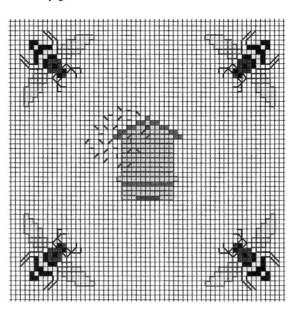

Making the honey pot cover

Mark corresponding centre lines both ways on the chart and the fabric. Using single thread and stitching over one intersection of fabric, work the beehive in the centre of the fabric (on a dark check). Then work the bees in the four corners (diagonally across the white checks). Outline using one thread. Hem narrow turnings around the cover. Press on the wrong side. Cover the honey pot, secure it first with an clastic band and then tie on the ribbon.

Paperweight

Materials

- 1 round glass paperweight, 8 cm (3 in) across
- 10 cm (4 in) square of 30 gauge white linen fabric
- DMC stranded embroidery cotton, 1 skein of each colour:

Pot
- pale blue 827
- blue 826
- dark blue 824
- blue-green 943, pot decoration with 1 thread
- outline 824

Plant
- pale green 955
- green 911
- dark green 909
- orange 741

Border
- 826, 741

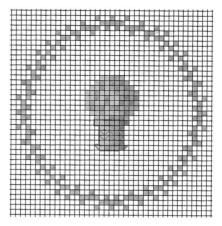

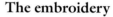

The embroidery

Using two threads, work the design in the middle of the fabric, stitching over two fabric threads. Outline with one thread. Press. Mount the embroidery into the paperweight following the manufacturer's instructions.

Box top

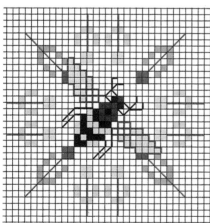

Materials

- 1 oval box 8 cm (3 in)
- 15 cm (6 in) square of 30 gauge off-white linen
- DMC stranded embroidery cotton, 1 skein of each colour:

Bee
- see page 40

Tulips
- yellow 725
- red 321
- pale green 913
- green 910
- dark green 890 for the stems

The embroidery

Work the design in the middle of the fabric, using two threads and cross stitching over two fabric threads. Press. Mount in the lid following the maker's instructions.

MAKING UP YOUR PROJECTS

Y OU WILL FIND THE FOLLOWING techniques useful for finishing the
hems of certain projects from slipstitch to open buttonhole.

Slipstitch

Slipstitch is almost invisible:
Use it on any fabric to neaten a
hem, stitching with a sewing
needle and matching thread.

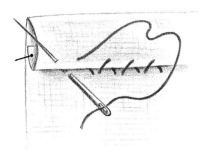

Hemstitch

This hem is particularly fine
and is most suitable for linen
tablemats. It is best used on
counted single thread fabrics.

• prepare the hem, as shown
• remove 2 or 3 threads along
the inside edge of the hem
• fold over and tack the hem
working close to the edge
• using a fine embroidery
needle, and a thread the same
thickness as the threads of the
fabric, work hemstitching as
shown in the diagram, to secure
the hem.

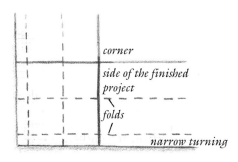

corner

side of the finished
project

folds

narrow turning

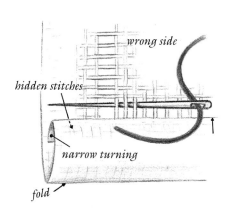

wrong side

hidden stitches

narrow turning

fold

wrong side

Frayed hem

Evenweave fabrics of all types can be finished in this way. A simple frayed hem is both unpretentious and quick to do.

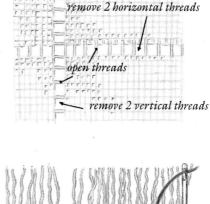

remove 2 horizontal threads

open threads

remove 2 vertical threads

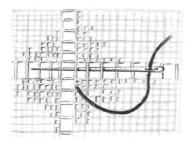

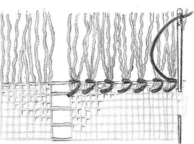

• Work out the desired length for the frayed hem
• remove 2 threads along the whole length
    • following the diagrams, hemstitch along the inside edge
• pull out the remaining threads to obtain the frayed hem.

Hem finished with bias binding

Instead of turning the hem to neaten, here the raw edges are covered with a bias-cut strip of fabric, in a matching or contrasting colour. If you prefer, choose the colour of the binding to offset your embroidery, using plain or patterned fabrics.
    • Place the bias strip on the seam allowance, right sides together and raw edges matching. Tack and stitch along the first fold then,
    • fold the binding over the raw edge to the wrong side. Turn under the second fold and tack in place:
    • using matching sewing thread, neatly slipstitch to finish.

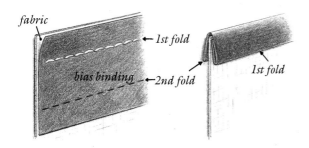

fabric

← 1st fold

bias binding ←2nd fold

1st fold

Buttonhole stitch border

Buttonhole stitch adds a decorative finish to an embroidered project, in either matching or contrasting thread. Work this stitch from left to right, as shown, bringing out the needle with the thread below.

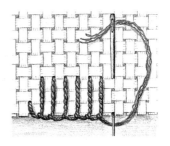

With this varied collection of projects, from seed sachets to a 'mummy bear' brooch, you will see that there are numerous opportunities for displaying your creative embroidery talents.

CONCLUSION

O NCE YOU HAVE WORKED THE individual motifs and the combined sampler, you will have a comprehensive understanding of how these cross stitch designs were created, using the garden as the basic theme.

In designing the projects, I hoped the reader would first be inspired to work them and then, using the information and ideas given, be able to continue successfully making his or her own creations.

My aim throughout the book has been to keep it simple and practical. In addition to giving step-by-step instructions for all stages of cross stitching and making up a project, I wanted to include a special feature on how to set about making your own designs and compositions – something I feel both beginners and experts often find challenging.

Some of the difficulty arises because embroidery is both a technique and an art (as in drawing and painting, which are freely expressed). To create does not mean that a project is invented in all respects – it may be that it is composed of a number of elements that already exist but, in putting them together, embroiderers may use their own individualistic style.

Remember also that existing patterns can be personalized by adding or changing certain motifs as well as the colour, for example, in much the same way as young girls used to do with their stitch samplers.

Sometimes, however, it is a great joy just to embroider, simply following another designer's instructions. This can be quite therapeutic and a restful pastime – as the photograph reassures us of the finished results, we know that the problems of colour, shape and balance, for example, have been resolved.

At the end of these exercises in cross stitch embroidery, I hope you will be sufficiently inspired to create your own imaginative designs, basing them either on further garden themes or subjects of your own choice. Garden styles alone offer an amazing variety of choice ranging, for example, from the country cottage to the grand and formal, and those specializing in botanical collections – whatever your choice, enjoy creating with cross stitch embroidery.

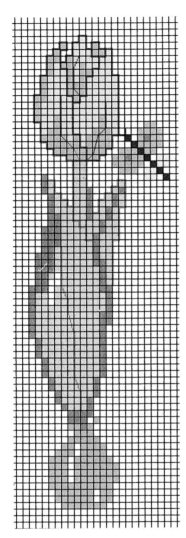

'Tulip' bookmark

This pretty pink tulip growing from its bulb, makes an ideal motif for a simple bookmark, which you can make using the materials supplied. For how to hemstitch and fray the edges, see page 43.

The embroidery

Embroider the motif in the centre of the fabric, see page 19. Using two strands in the needle, work each stitch over one block. Outline using one strand.

Materials
- 1 rectangle of 12 gauge Aida fabric
- DMC stranded embroidery cotton, 1 skein of each colour:
- pale pink 776
- pink 3712
- dark pink 309
- ochre 783
- green 3348
- olive green 3012
- pale blue 747
- blue 519
- dark blue 3750
- white

Acknowledgements

I would like to thank DMC, especially Corinne Valette
without whose contribution and support this book
would not have been possible.

Thank you to Christine Certain for her help.

I would also like to thank the DMC creative department,
Isabelle Fauquet, Veronique Enginger and Christine Pique
for their advice and the design of the charts.

Finally, I am grateful to my husband and my children
for their support and patience.

Premiere Page would like to thank Dominique Artigaud,
Laurence Bulle and Jean-Noël Mouret for
the production of the book.

The threads, fabrics and accessories used in this
book are manufactured by DMC.

*Photocopy the following 16 pages to assemble the complete chart for the large
sampler on pages 36–37. Page XII contains the charts for the leeks, pumpkin
and lettuce on page 23, and for the rabbit (page 29).*

Symbol	DMC	Note	Group
•	white		
Ė	natural		
▣	739		beige
✕	644		
	640	d	
7	744		yellow
o	742		orange
+	741		
✕	740		
s	972		
▼	971		
ω	402		brown
Ψ	921		
ε	918	h	
	783	m	
≠	729		
∖	437		
c	435		
◆	780		
◆	976		
▽	975	g	
∅	433	n	
●	801	t	
	938	r	
ⱷ	3772		
	632	u	
	3685	b	pink/red
/	3350		
6	326		
∠	321	∅	
÷	3733		
c	554		violet
Y	208		
∝	3746		
I	809		blue
	798	f	
∪	827		
–	826		
ɕ	824		
∖	747		in half-stitch
	943	g	green
T	993		
8	992		
◢	991		
	500	s	
◇	955		
⋈	911		
/	909	k	
∨	704		
⌄	702		
∅	700	a	
⊣	699		
⊙	369		
z	472		
	471	j	
✕	470		
▲	937	h	
/	320		
⊘	319		
	890	i	
+	3348		
3	3347		
=	3346		
⊘	3345		
◆	895		
%	907		
◎	906		
L	904	l	
∖	762		grey
□	414	c	
∕	415		
▣	3799	e	
■	noir	N	

I

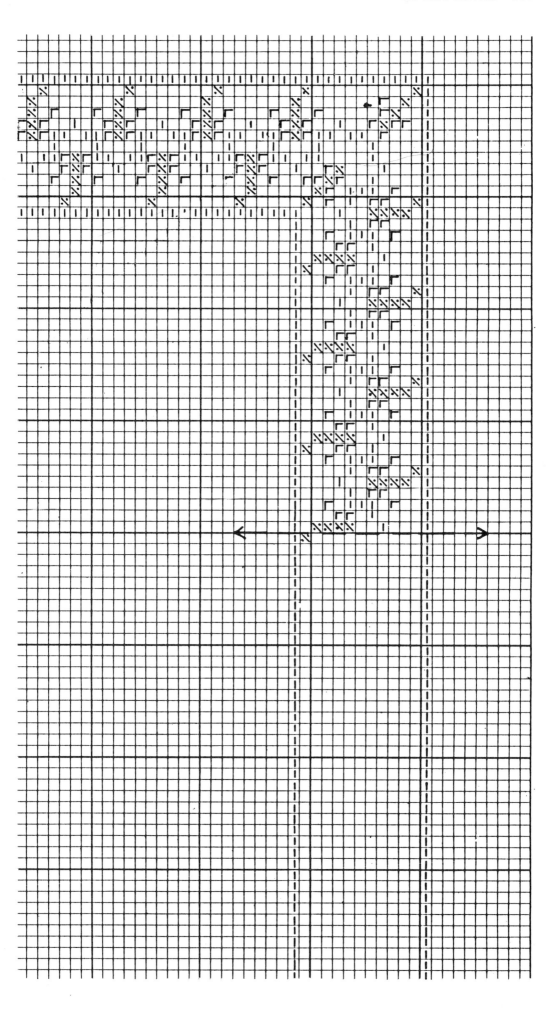

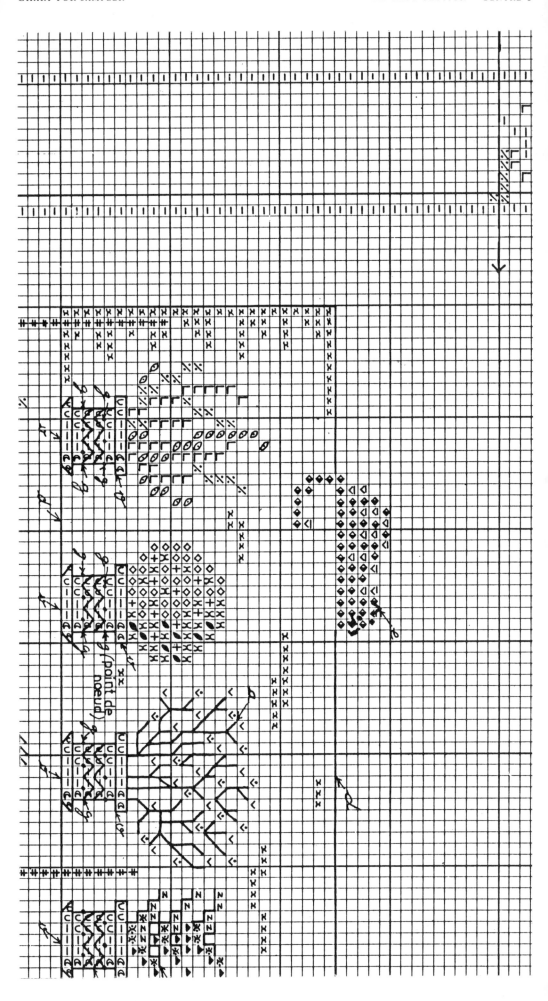

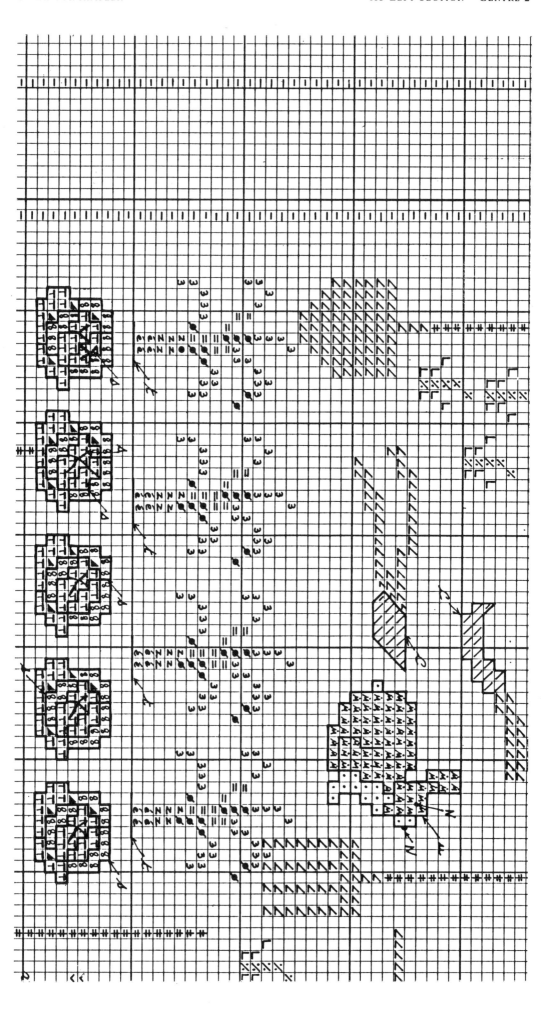

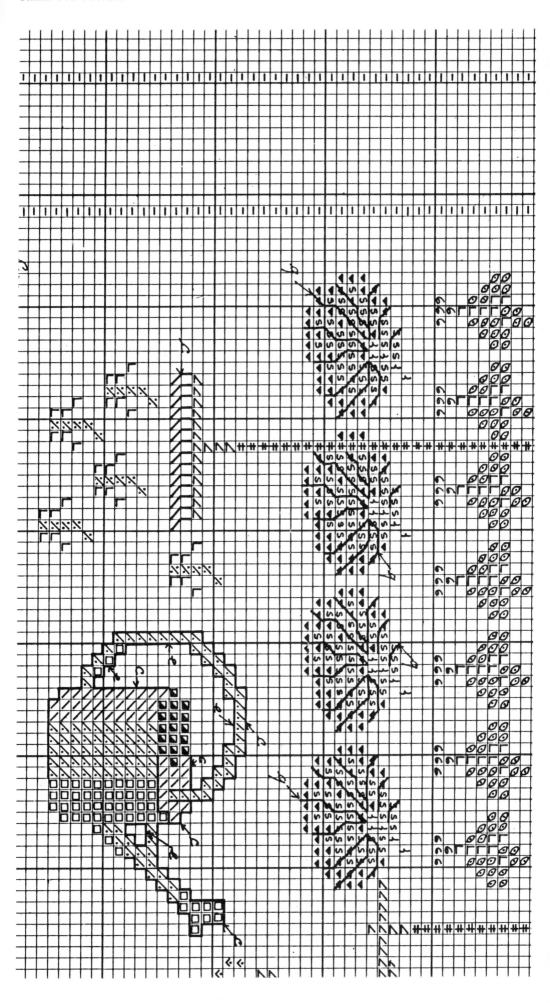

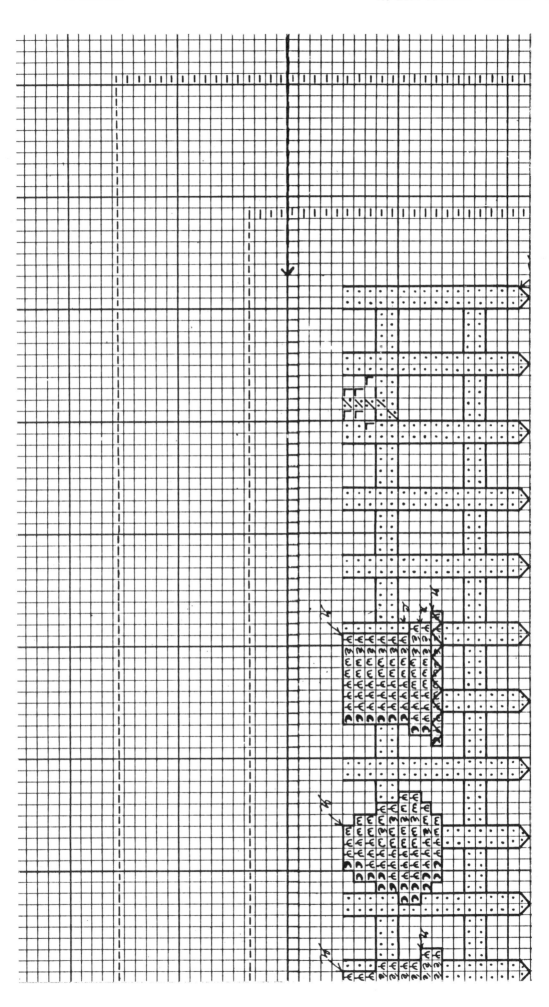

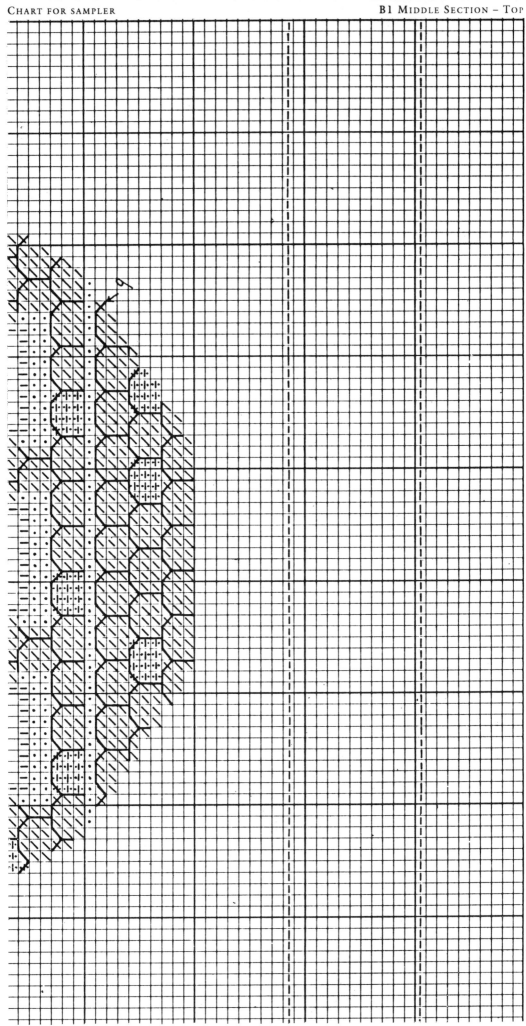

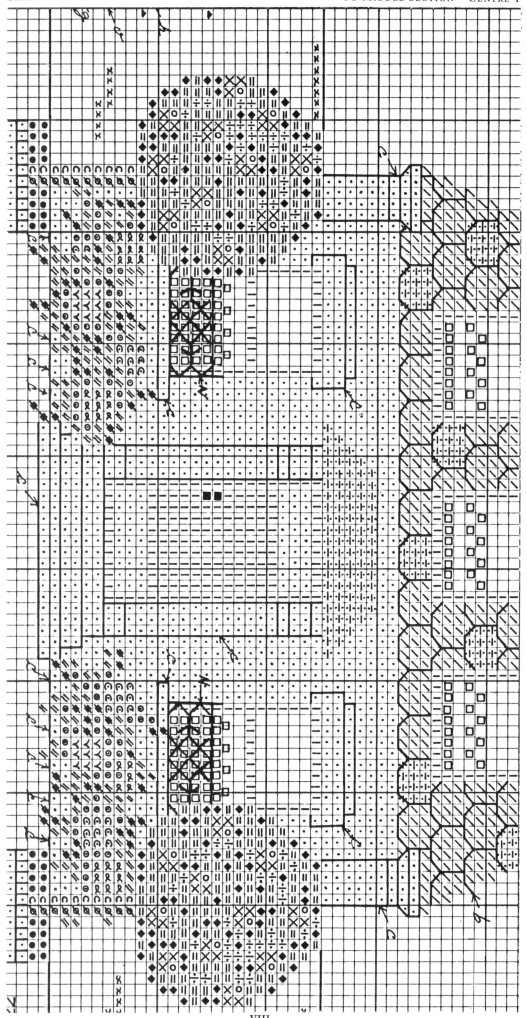

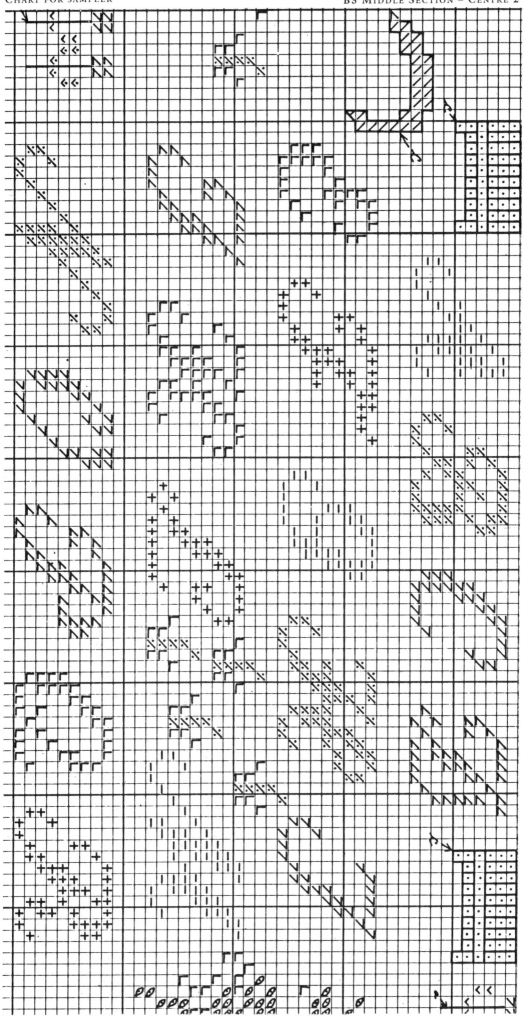

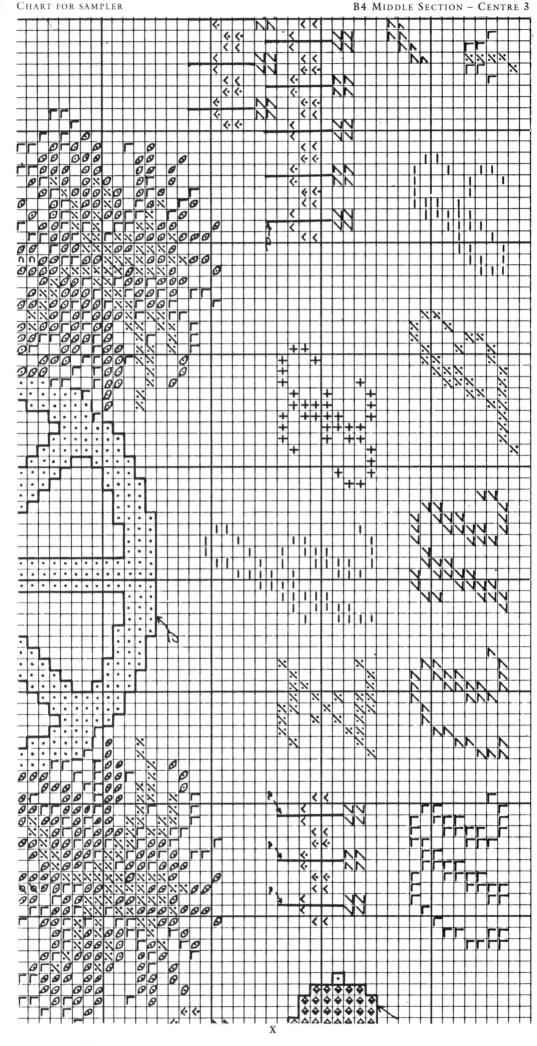

X

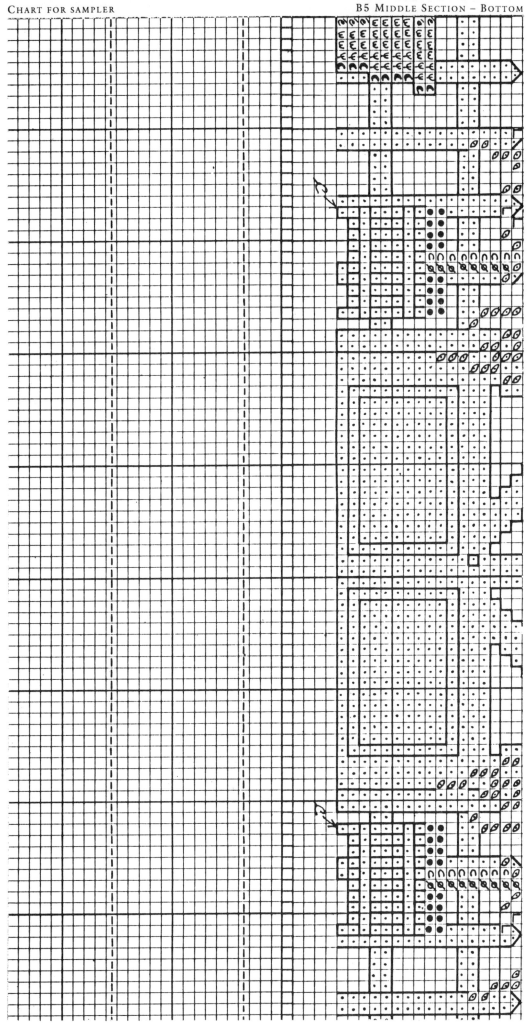

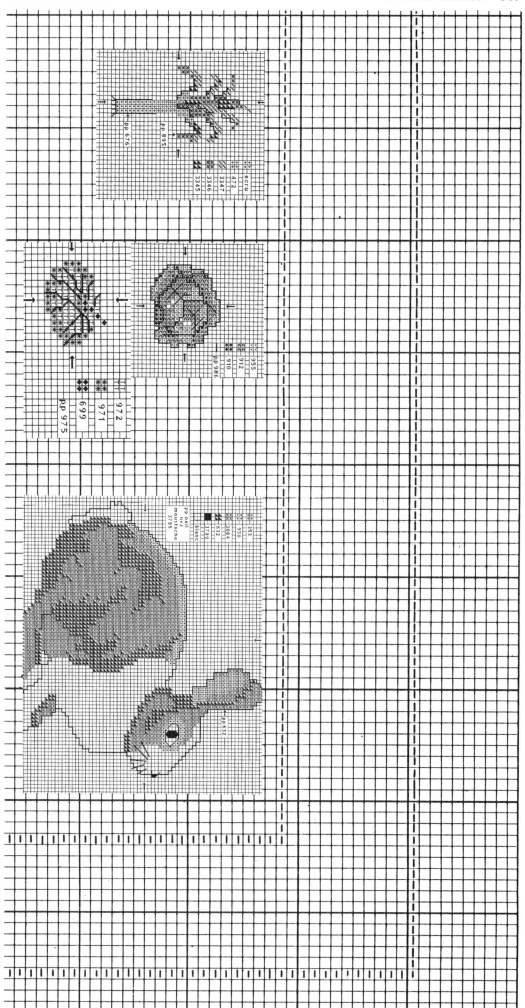

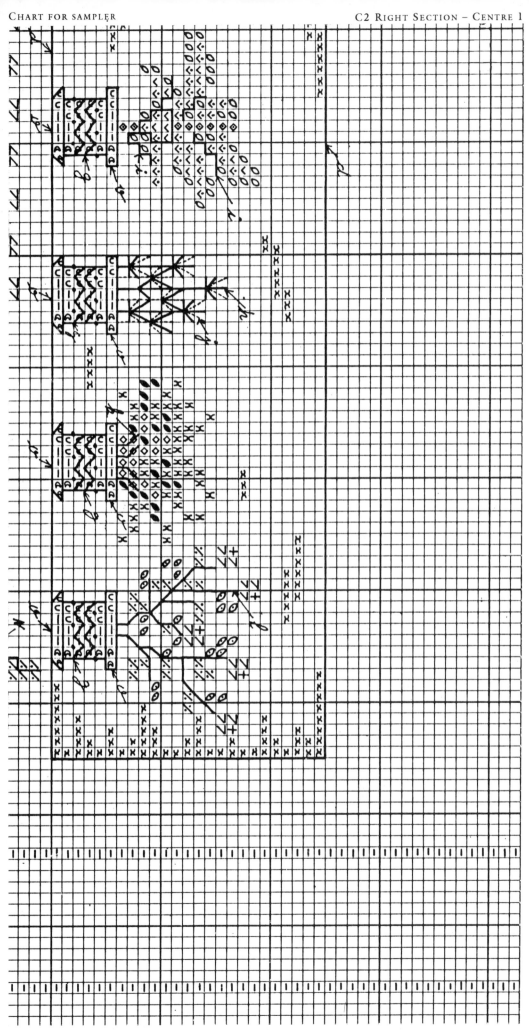

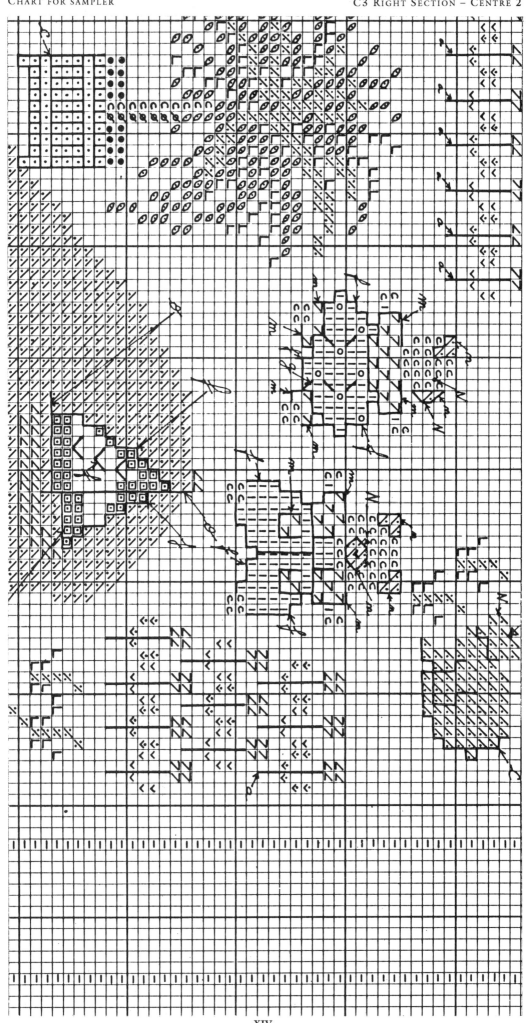

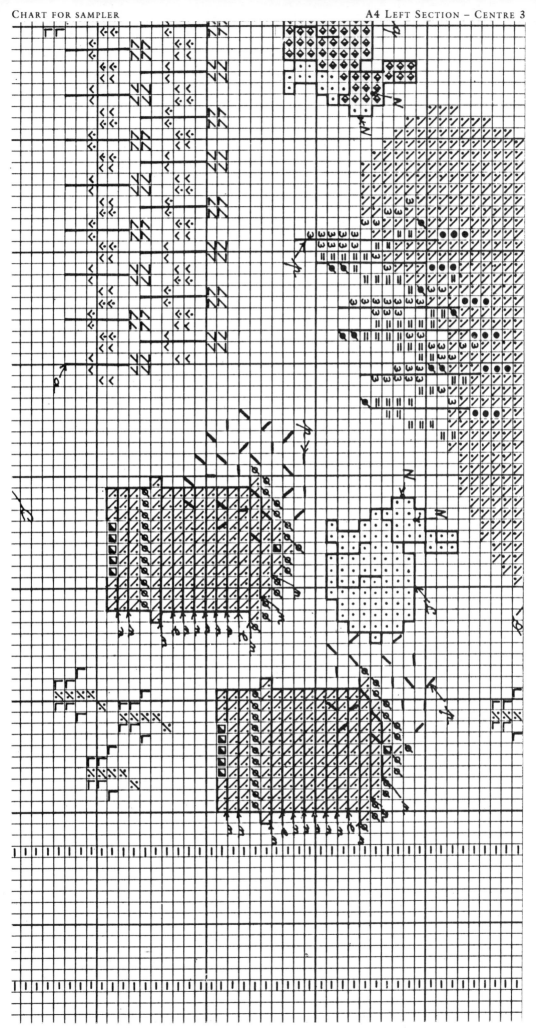

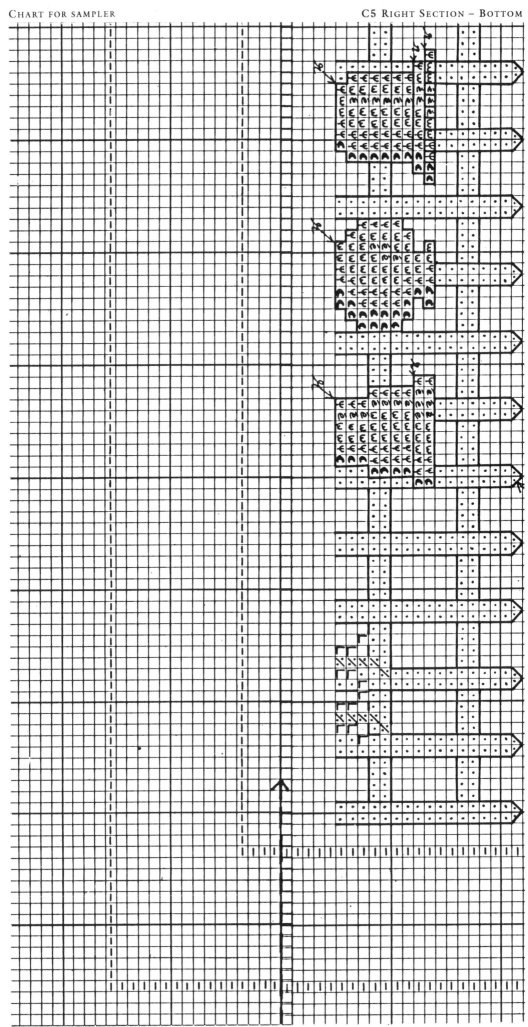

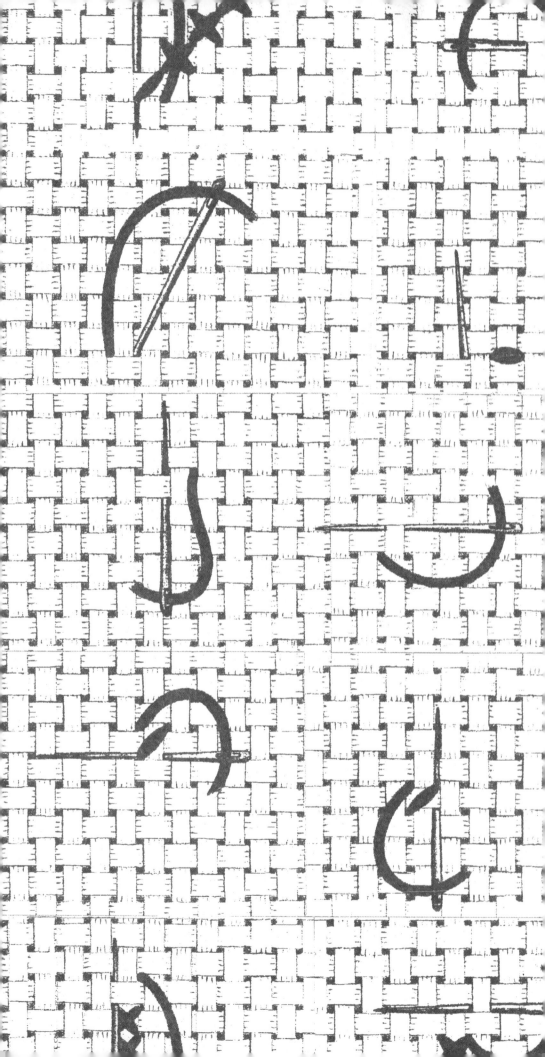